Machines Inside Machines

Using Screws

Wendy Sadler

www.raintreepublishers.co.uk
Visit our website to find out more information about **Raintree** books.

To order:
☎ Phone 44 (0) 1865 888112
▤ Send a fax to 44 (0) 1865 314091
▢ Visit the Raintree Bookshop at **www.raintreepublishers.co.uk** to browse our catalogue and order online.

First published in Great Britain by Raintree, Halley Court, Jordan Hill, Oxford, OX2 8EJ, part of Harcourt Education.
Raintree is a registered trademark of Harcourt Education Ltd.

Editorial: Melanie Copland and Kate Buckingham
Design: Michelle Lisseter, Victoria Bevan and Bridge Creative Services Ltd
Picture Research: Hannah Taylor
Production: Duncan Gilbert

Originated by Repro Multi Warna
Printed and bound in China by South China Printing Company

ISBN 1 844 43605 5
09 08 07 06 05
10 9 8 7 6 5 4 3 2 1

British Library Cataloguing in Publication Data
Sadler, Wendy
Using Screws. – (Machines Inside Machines)
621.8'82
A full catalogue record for this book is available from the British Library.

Acknowledgements
The publishers would like to thank the following for permission to reproduce photographs:
Alamy Images (Justin Kase) p. 16; Corbis (Sygma/ Jacques Langevin) p. 25; Corbis (Scott T. Smith) p. 17; DK Images p. 27; FLPA (Minden Pictures/ Flip Nicklin) pp. 28–29; Getty Images (Photodisc) p. 12; Getty Images (The Image Bank) p. 19; Harcourt Education Ltd (Peter Morris) p. 5; Harcourt Education Ltd (Trevor Clifford) pp. 22, 24; Harcourt Education Ltd (Tudor Photography) pp. 4, 6, 7, 8, 10, 11, 14, 15, 21, 23, 26; Rex Features pp. 9, 13; Science Photo Library (Martin Bond) p. 18.

Cover photograph of screws reproduced with permission of Alamy Images/ Tom Mareschal.

Every effort has been made to contact copyright holders of any material reproduced in this book. Any omissions will be rectified in subsequent printings if notice is given to the publishers.

The paper used to print this book comes from sustainable resources

Any words appearing in the text in bold,
like this, are explained in the glossary.

Machines that use screws

Screws can be used to hold things together. Have a look around you. How many things can you see that might be held together by screws? Sometimes screws are hidden inside things, so you cannot see them. Lots of different machines have got screws inside them.

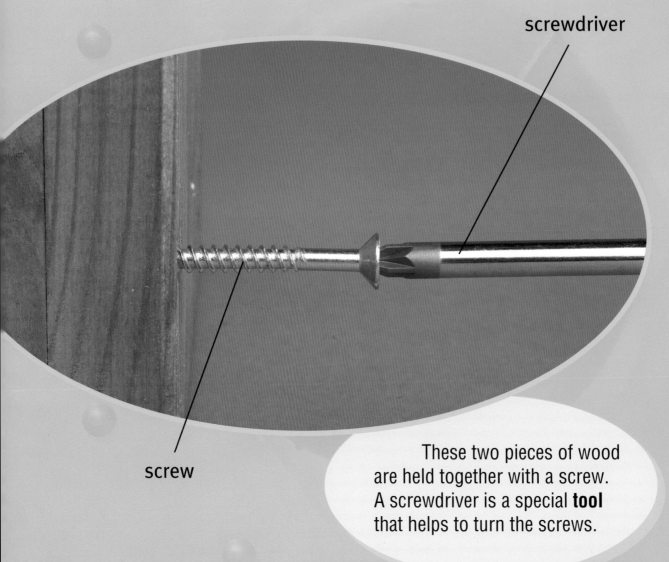

screwdriver

screw

These two pieces of wood are held together with a screw. A screwdriver is a special **tool** that helps to turn the screws.

Lifting and squeezing

Screws can also be used to lift things up – even water! Some screws can move **material** and make huge holes in the ground. Screws can also **squeeze** things together really tightly. Screws are very simple, but very important.

This tool is called a vice. It holds things very tightly. The screw in the middle moves the jaws together to grip an object.

screw

jaws

object

vice

A screw is a **simple machine**. This is something that makes a job easier to do. A screw is made of a **ramp** wrapped around a pole or spike. A ramp is a piece of material in the shape of a **slope**. It is also called an **inclined plane**. Screws can be very small or very big.

Activity

1. Take a triangle of paper and a pencil. The sloping side of the triangle should be longer than the pencil.

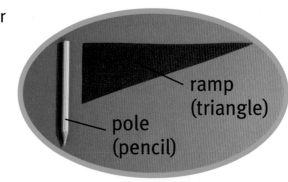

ramp (triangle)

pole (pencil)

2. Roll the paper around the pencil. Can you see how the ramp (paper triangle) and pole (pencil) turn into a screw shape?

The pencil has a point at the end called a **wedge**. This wedge shape is often found on screws. It gives a sharp point to make holes in **material**.

Changing movement

A screw can change turning movements into forwards and backwards or up and down movements. When you unscrew the lid from a drink bottle you turn it round. As you do this, the lid moves upwards. The screw has changed the direction of movement.

A bottle top is a screw you can turn with your hands. Some screws need a special **tool**, called a screwdriver, to turn them.

The screwdriver fits into the screw. As you turn the screwdriver, the screw also turns and moves downwards into the material.

Have another look at the screw shape you made from a pencil and paper. The longest side, or **slope**, of the triangle is the **ramp** of the screw.

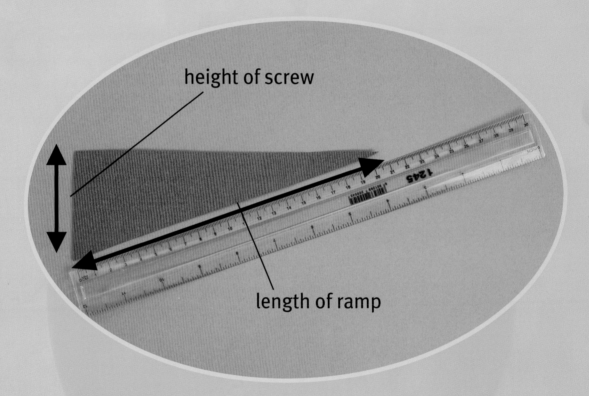

height of screw

length of ramp

The ramp of a screw is always longer than the height of the screw. To drive a screw into a wall it is turned round and round many times to move forwards a short distance. It must be turned until it has moved around the same distance as the length of the ramp.

Up and down

Screw shapes can also be used to get up or down a steep hill. Going round and round means you put in less effort but over a longer distance. The length of the slope around the screw is much longer than the height you need to climb.

Because they are walking around a slope, these people need less **effort force** to climb to each level of the building.

The **thread** is the name for the **ramp** that wraps around the pole of the screw. On some screws you can see lots of lines around the sides. These screws have a **fine thread**. If you could unwrap the ramp it would be very long. Fine thread screws have to be turned lots of times to move them into a **material**. These screws are used if you have a very hard material to screw into. You would need lots of turns, but each one would need only a little **effort force**.

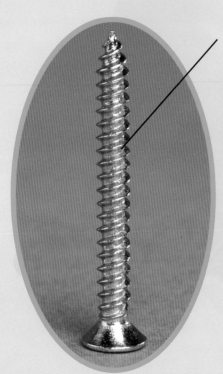

A fine thread screw has lots of lines and a long ramp.

A coarse thread screw has few lines and a short ramp.

Coarse thread screws

Some screws have a short ramp around them, which winds its way up the screw more steeply than on a fine thread screw. This is called a **coarse thread** and there are very few lines around the sides of the screw. These screws are used for making holes in soft materials.

The screw holding this dog's lead in the ground has a coarse thread because the soil is soft.

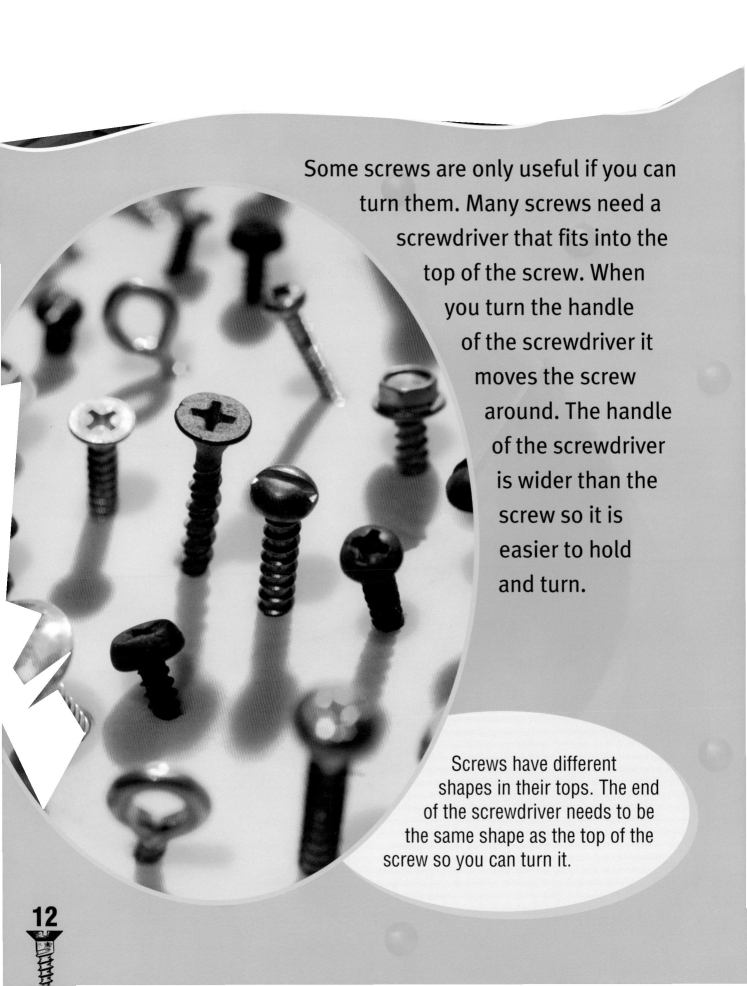

Some screws are only useful if you can turn them. Many screws need a screwdriver that fits into the top of the screw. When you turn the handle of the screwdriver it moves the screw around. The handle of the screwdriver is wider than the screw so it is easier to hold and turn.

Screws have different shapes in their tops. The end of the screwdriver needs to be the same shape as the top of the screw so you can turn it.

Special shapes

Some machines have screws with very unusual shapes in the top. Screws like this are often used in computer games machines to stop people taking them apart. If you do not have the right shape screwdriver, it is very hard to get these screws out.

Computer games machines like this one often use unusually shaped screw tops to stop people taking them apart.

What would happen without...?

It is impossible to unscrew most screws using just your fingers because the screws are small and difficult to hold on to. Screwdrivers make it much easier!

Screws can be different shapes for using with different **materials**. A wood screw, for example, is like a **wedge** with **sloping** sides most of the way up. This means it can be screwed into wood without **drilling** a hole first. As the screw turns, it makes its own hole in the wood.

Wood screws can be screwed straight into wood without drilling a hole first.

Nuts and bolts

A **bolt** has straight sides and needs a **nut** to hold it in place. The nut is a circle-shaped piece of metal or plastic with a **thread** on the inside. It matches up with the thread on the outside of the bolt.

A nut and bolt can only be used if you can reach both sides of the material you want to join.

A bolt is put through a hole on one side of a piece of material. The end of the bolt sticks out on the other side. The nut screws on to the bolt to hold it in place.

Playing on giant screws

Some fairground slides have a **ramp** that is wrapped around a cone shape. It is a bit like a giant, upside-down screw. The distance you travel down the slide is further than the height of the cone. You travel a lot more slowly on the slide than if you went straight down the side of the cone!

Sliding down a helter-skelter feels like you are going very fast, but the ramp is actually helping to slow you down!

cone shape

ramp that you slide down

Water slide

Some swimming pools have slides that are like giant screws. The slide tube is wrapped around a metal frame. When you slide down inside the tube the water makes the slide slippery. Without the water, there would be **friction** between you and the slide. Friction happens when two surfaces rub together. The water means there is less friction, so you slide down more smoothly. This means you go faster!

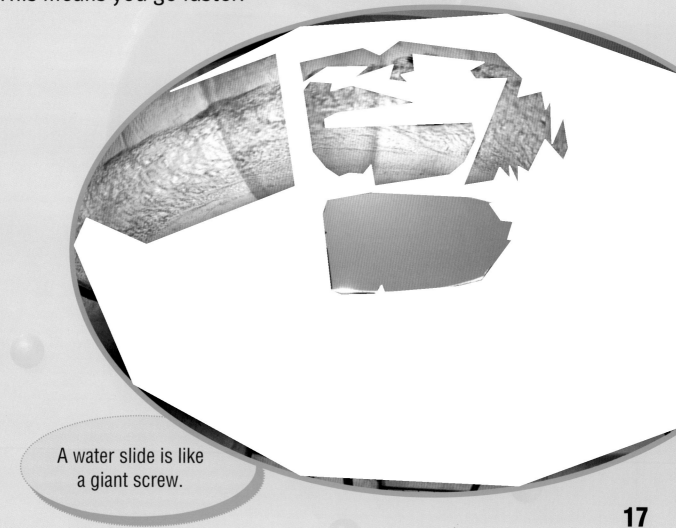

A water slide is like a giant screw.

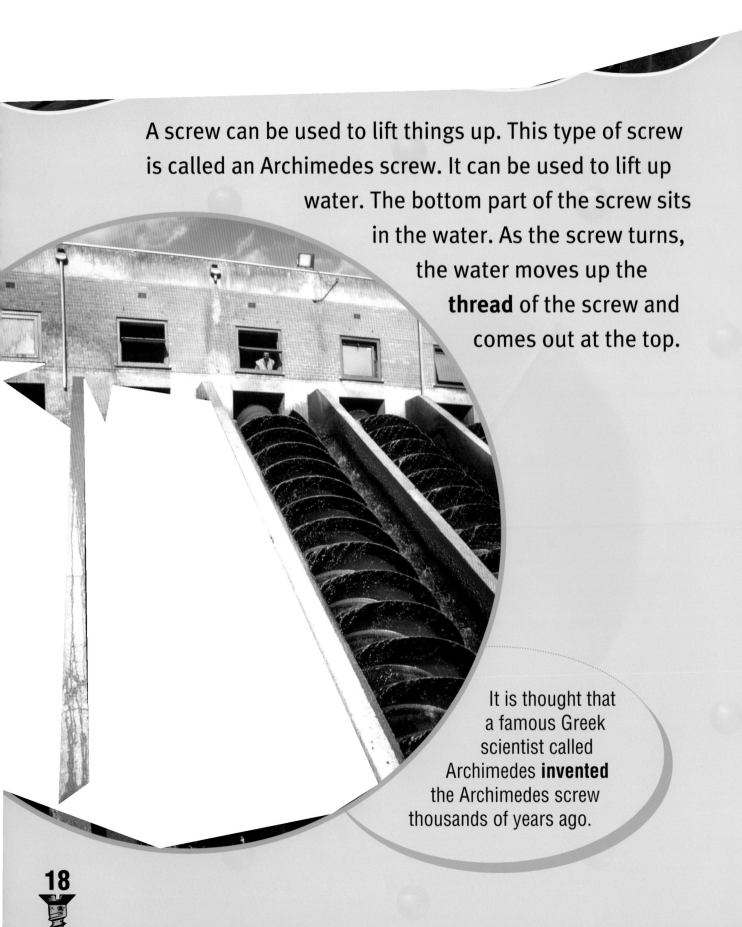

A screw can be used to lift things up. This type of screw is called an Archimedes screw. It can be used to lift up water. The bottom part of the screw sits in the water. As the screw turns, the water moves up the **thread** of the screw and comes out at the top.

It is thought that a famous Greek scientist called Archimedes **invented** the Archimedes screw thousands of years ago.

A similar machine, called a screw conveyor, can be used to move flour or grain in factories. The screw conveyor sits in a container of grain. As the screw turns, the grain is moved along the machine to another part of the factory. Screw conveyors are a very simple way of moving dry **material** around.

If all this grain had to be moved around the factory by hand it would take a very long time.

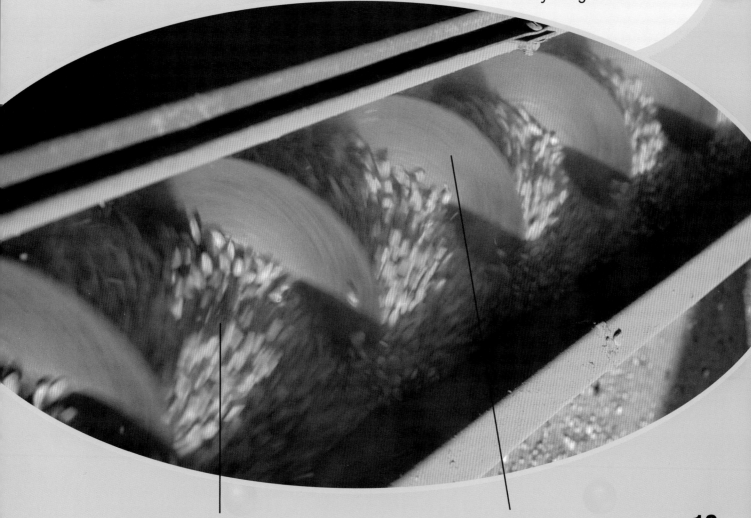

grain moved as blades turn   blades of screw

Many taps are turned on and off with the help of a screw. The screw is hidden inside the tap. When you turn the tap on you are undoing the screw. As the screw turns round you are moving a part of the tap, called a washer, upwards.

How does a tap work?

Inside the tap, the screw moves the washer up and down. When you turn the tap on, the screw lifts the washer up and lets the water flow out. When you turn the tap off, the screw pushes the washer down and stops the water getting out.

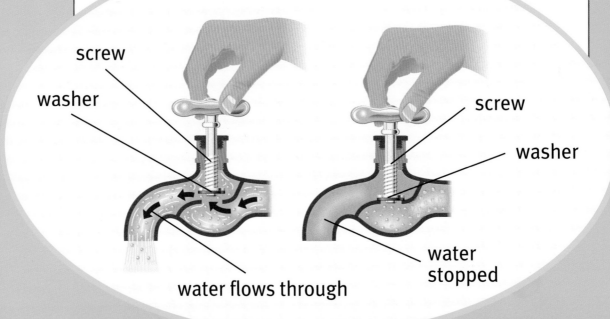

screw

washer

water flows through

screw

washer

water stopped

Lids and things!

Many bottles, jars and tubes in your home will have screw tops. Fizzy drink bottles have screw tops. You need to turn the screw lid up tight to make sure it keeps the fizz in.

lid thread

jar thread

The **thread** on the jar has an opposite pattern to the thread on the lid. This means that they will screw together neatly to keep the jar shut tight.

Screws can be used together with another **simple machine** called a **cog**. A cog is a wheel that has teeth around the edge. A screw and a cog together are called a **worm gear**.

When you turn the screw the **ramp** pushes against the teeth of the cog. This makes the cog turn in a different direction from the screw.

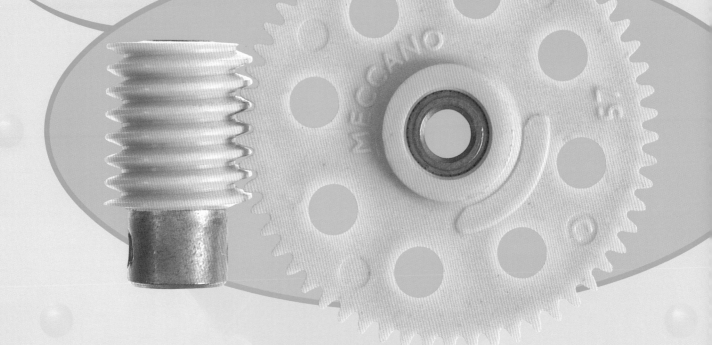

A worm gear helps you to change the speed and direction of a movement. If you turn the screw the cog will move slowly. If you turn the cog you can make the screw move around very fast.

Activity

A kitchen hand whisk uses a worm gear. If you have one in your kitchen, have a close look at it. Can you see where the screw is? When you turn the handle, do you turn the cog or the screw?

A whisk is a machine made of more than one simple machine. This means we call it a **compound machine**.

cog

whisk blades turn

turn handle

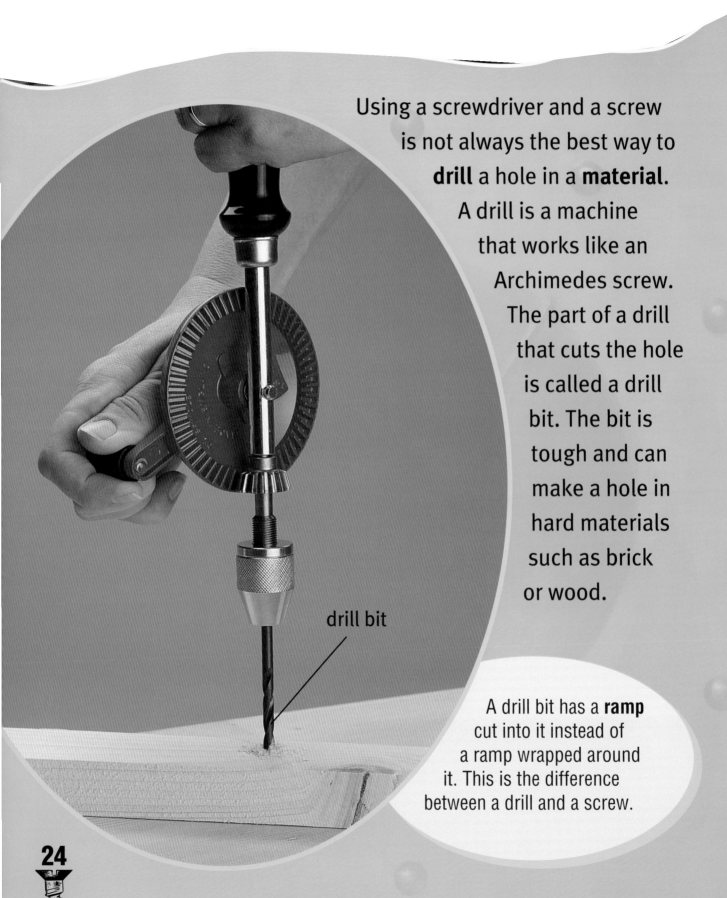

Using a screwdriver and a screw is not always the best way to **drill** a hole in a **material**. A drill is a machine that works like an Archimedes screw. The part of a drill that cuts the hole is called a drill bit. The bit is tough and can make a hole in hard materials such as brick or wood.

drill bit

A drill bit has a **ramp** cut into it instead of a ramp wrapped around it. This is the difference between a drill and a screw.

Giant drills

If you had a giant drill you could make really big holes! Between Britain and France there is a huge tunnel called the Channel Tunnel. It runs through rock under the sea that separates the two countries. This tunnel was made by a huge drilling machine.

This is the giant drilling machine that was used to make the Channel Tunnel.

A corkscrew is a **compound machine** you might find in your kitchen. The screw that goes into the cork is joined to two arms at the side. When the screw twists into the cork, the arms are pushed up. The arms are joined to the screw with **cogs**. When you push the arms down, the cogs turn. This pulls the screw upwards, lifting the cork with it.

How do you think you would get a cork out of a bottle without a corkscrew?

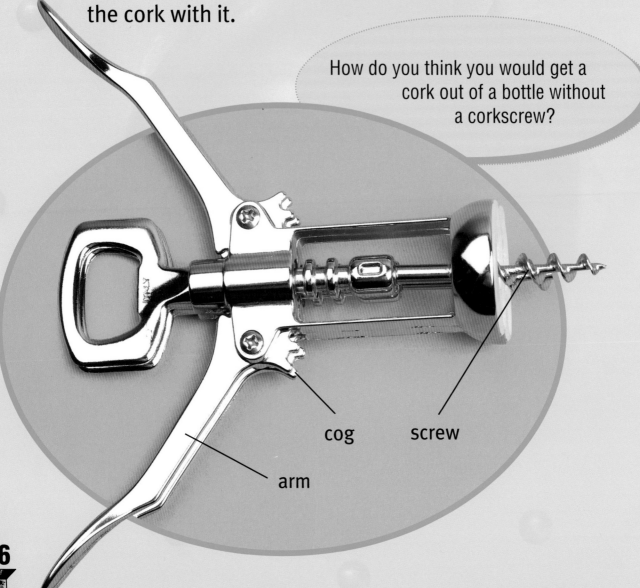

cog   screw

arm

Screws can be used to **adjust** things. Chairs and stools that have screws can be adjusted to the right height.

Some **tools** can also be adjusted using screws. A wrench is a tool that holds on to **bolts** to undo them. The part of the wrench that holds on to the bolt can be made larger or smaller to fit big and little bolts. A wheel turns a screw to move the sides of the wrench in and out.

The seat of this stool is on the end of a screw. If you turn the screw you can change the height of the stool.

screw

Some scientists in Japan have made tiny swimming robots. These robots use spinning screw-shaped tails to swim around inside the human body! When the tail spins it pushes the robot forwards. Scientists hope that in the future these robots will be able to repair things inside people's bodies.

This is a narwhal. Can you see the screw shape on the front tooth?

A narwhal is a strange type of whale with a long spiral top tooth. This tooth can grow to more than 2 metres long! The tooth is shaped just like a screw. Scientists do not really know why the tooth grows into this shape. Some people think it is because some parts of the tooth grow too fast so they have to curl around. What do you think?

You can find out about **simple machines** by talking to your teacher or parents. Think about the simple machines you use every day – how do you think they work? Your local library will have books and information about this. You will find the answers to many of your questions in this book, but you can also use other books and the Internet.

Books to read

Science Around Us: Using Machines, Sally Hewitt
    (Chrysalis Children's Books, 2004)
Very Useful Machines: Screws, Chris Oxlade
    (Heinemann Library, 2003)

Using the Internet

Explore the Internet to find out more about screws. Try using a search engine such as www.yahooligans.com or www.internet4kids.com, and type in keywords such as 'screws', '**ramp**', and '**bolts**'.

adjust change something slightly to make it right for a certain job

bolt long screw with no point at the end. Nuts screw on to bolts to hold them in place.

coarse thread lines around the edge of a screw that are far apart

compound machine machine that uses two or more simple machines

cog wheel with teeth around the edge

drill make a hole

effort force force that you put into a screw

fine thread lines around the edge of a screw that are close together

friction something that happens when two surfaces rub against each other. Friction can slow things down or stop them moving.

inclined plane sloping surface or ramp

invent to discover or make something for the first time

material substance that can be used to make things. Wood, brick, plastic and paper are all examples of materials.

nut metal shape with a hole in the middle. On the inside edges of the hole is a thread to screw it on to a bolt.

ramp sloping surface

simple machine something that can change the effort force needed to move something, or change the direction it moves in

slope ramp shaped surface. The side of a hill or a car park ramp may be slopes.

squeeze push something together tightly from all sides

thread lines around the edge of a screw

tool something that helps us to do a certain job. A screwdriver is a tool that helps us to tighten screws.

wedge two ramps joined together, back to back

worm gear screw and cog working together